D1717016

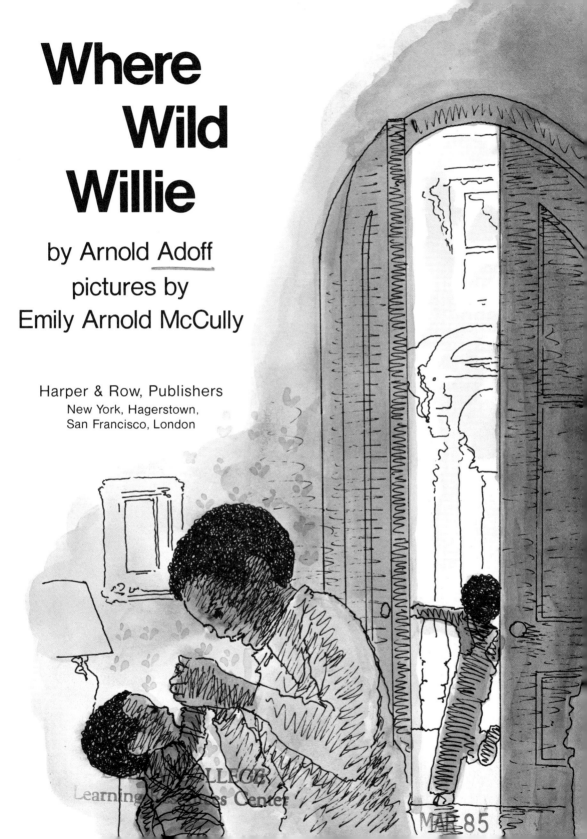

Where
Wild
Willie

by Arnold Adoff

pictures by
Emily Arnold McCully

Harper & Row, Publishers
New York, Hagerstown,
San Francisco, London

Library of Congress Cataloging in Publication Data
Adoff, Arnold.
    Where wild Willie

    SUMMARY: A young girl fantasizes about the excitement
and loneliness of running away.
    1. Runaway children—Juvenile poetry. [1. Runaways
—Poetry] I. McCully, Emily Arnold. II. Title.
PZ8.3.A233Wh   76-21390
ISBN 0-06-020092-8
ISBN 0-06-020093-6 lib. bdg.

for
    jaime
     ellen
charlotte
    leigh
and
all the
girl
    and
     boy
   willies
be
    in
free

one
  warm
  wednesday

  willie
  walked a
            way

  want to run

  want to
              say

  wild
  willie

  stay

we
    want
    willie

    home
        to
   stay

      home
         for
         dinner
      home
        to
         play

   want
   willie
   home

   wild
   willie
     play

willie
   hide
    here
willie
   hide
    there

     willie
     can
      hide
     out
     any
      where

wild
willie
   here

where
willie

   there

9

where
        wild
        willie

        can
        you
        see

willie see you
willie see
                me

        wild
        willie

        where
        willie

                she

willie
    in   the
    basement
willie
    down
      the
      hall

      willie
      in the
      back
      yard
  ten
  feet
   tall

willie
    wild
    willie

don't
fall

willie
    o
willie

      come
      home

    to
        me

willie
      wild
willie

      to
      me

willie
    can hide
    the
       whole
    day long

      willie is smart
      willie is
          strong

where
willie

wild
willie

   look
   long

where
>   wild
>   willie

>   walk
>   in
>   the
>   street

>   where wild
>   willie
>   with
>   the
>   whisper
>   in
>   feet

>   willie
>   wild
>   willie

>   street
>   feet

17

willie
   at the
   window

   look
      in
   in
    the
   house

      willie
        in the
     dark place
  quiet
  as
  a
  mouse

willie
  wild
willie

  house
  mouse

where
    wild
    willie

    walk
            in
that
        way

            willie
                is
                a
        shadow
on a
sun
        shine
day

    shadow
            willie
    shadow

            play

willie
      in   a
    dark
    place

    keep
        in
   out of
    sight

      willie
      with
        a
     warm
     face
wait
     in
for
    the
   night

wild
willie

willie
    in a
  dark
  place
willie
    in the
     light

      willie
        is
        a
     strange
      face
slip
   in
through
   the
 night

willie
  where
willie

  shine
  light

where
     wild
     willie

    in the
      cold
      cold
      night

        willie
        come
        home
  let us
    hug
you
    tight

willie
     wild
     willie

     will
     you

willie

    o

willie

    the long

      night

     through

willie

  is

  me

    and

willie

  is

  you

wild

willie

    o

willie

   love

   you

willie
    is you
willie
    is me

   willie
     is
com
   in
home
   to
  be

wild
willie

willie
      wild
      willie

        be
      free
      be
      free

willie

wild

willie

be

free

Child Lit.
PZ
8.3
.A233   Adoff, Arnold.
Wh   Where wild Willie / by Arnold Adoff ;
           pictures by Emily Arnold McCully. --
           1st ed. -- New York : Harper & Row,
           c1978.

    PB   31 p. : col. ill. ; 24 cm.

               ISBN 0-06-020092-8 : $5.95. ISBN 0-
           06-020093-6 lib. bdg. : $6.79

               1.Runaway children--Juvenile poetry.
           I.McCully, Emily Arnold. II.Title.

PZ8.3.A233Wh   811

                                    76-21390
                                    MARC AC